JOHN THOMPSON'S
EASIEST PIANO COURSE

PART FIVE

PLAYBACK+
Speed • Pitch • Balance • Loop

To access audio, visit:
www.halleonard.com/mylibrary

Enter Code
5214-4085-6038-0230

ISBN 978-1-4584-9118-3

EXCLUSIVELY DISTRIBUTED BY

© 1956 by The Willis Music Co.
International Copyright Secured All Rights Reserved

No part of this publication may be reproduced in any form or by
any means without the prior written permission of the Publisher.

Visit Hal Leonard Online at
www.halleonard.com

Contact Us:
Hal Leonard
7777 West Bluemound Road
Milwaukee, WI 53213
Email: info@halleonard.com

In Europe, contact:
Hal Leonard Europe Limited
42 Wigmore Street
Marylebone, London, W1U 2RN
Email: info@halleonardeurope.com

In Australia, contact:
Hal Leonard Australia Pty. Ltd.
4 Lentara Court
Cheltenham, Victoria, 3192 Australia
Email: info@halleonard.com.au

Foreword

SCOPE

The material in PART FIVE presents the following:

Sixteenth notes in Two-Four, Three-Four, Four-Four and Six-Eight

Leger Lines above the Treble Staff.

Leger Lines below the Bass Staff.

Grace Notes.

Elementary use of the Pedal.

The Legato Pedal in chord playing.

Thumb under second and third fingers.

Second and third fingers over thumb.

Transposition.

Further studies in Syncopation.

REVIEW WORK

As in the earlier books of this Course, plenty of review material is given so that the pupil has ample opportunity to develop each new point learned.

This is especially so in regard to technical matters such as passing the thumb under and the hand over—a most important detail of technic. The material also provides for the use of staccato and legato touches, learned earlier in the Course.

It is most important that these touches be applied exactly as marked as they form a vital part of Interpretation.

THE PEDAL

Use of the Pedal has been indicated rather sparingly—only in the more obvious places. For those pupils who show more aptitude in its use additional markings may be made at the discretion of the teacher.

ARTISTRY AND MUSICIANSHIP

The prime purpose in teaching this book should be that of having the pupil play *as musically as possible*. Every effort should be directed toward this end.

Try also to develop a general increase in Tempo—but never at the expense of accuracy.

In the following books, the material becomes slightly more advanced both musically and pianistically.

John Thompson

Contents

	Page
FOREWORD	4
SIXTEENTH NOTES IN THREE-FOUR "When Knighthood Was in Flower"	5
SYNCOPATION "Westward Ho!"	6
LEGER LINES (Chart)	7
LEGER LINES BELOW BASS STAFF "Dance of the Hobgoblins"	8
GRACE NOTES "The Campbells Are Coming"	10
STACCATO PLAYING from "The Magic Flute" W. A. Mozart	12
PEDAL STUDY	13
BROKEN CHORDS WITH PEDAL "Over the Fence is Out!"	14
THE PEDAL IN CHORD PLAYING "The Church Organ"	16
RAPID TWO-NOTE SLURS "Fun On the Beach"	17
REVIEW PIECE from "The Emperor Waltz" J. Strauss	18
REVIEW PIECE "Through the Clouds"	20
SIXTEENTHS IN FOUR-FOUR "Etude"	22
SIXTEENTHS IN TWO-FOUR "The Lonesome Stream"	22
SIXTEENTHS IN SIX-EIGHT "Etude"	23
REVIEW PIECE "Serenade"	23
BROKEN CHORDS WITH PEDAL "Old Faithful Geyser"	24
REVIEW PIECE "The New Bike"	26
THUMB UNDER AND 2nd FINGER OVER "Etude"	27
REVIEW PIECE "Whirling Propellers"	28
THUMB UNDER 3rd FINGER "Etude"	29
3rd FINGER OVER THUMB "Ballet Rehearsal"	30
REVIEW PIECE "In the Days of Powdered Wigs"	32
LEGATO AND STACCATO CONTRAST "The Tobacco Auctioneer"	33
LEGER LINES ABOVE TREBLE STAFF "Music Box"	34
TRANSPOSITION "Barn Dance"	36
THE DOUBLE FLAT "Black Key Rag"	37
REVIEW PIECE "The Caissons Go Rolling Along"	38
REVIEW PIECE from "Danube Waves" J. Ivanovici	40
STUDY IN RHYTHM "Tango"	42
CHORD PLAYING (Forearm Attack) "The School Song"	43
RECITAL PIECE from "Spring Song" F. Mendelssohn	44
CERTIFICATE OF MERIT	47

Sixteenth Notes
(In Three-Four)

A SIXTEENTH note has a full head, a stem and two hooks. It looks like this, ♬

It has half the value of an 8th note, therefore there are two 16ths to one 8th note.

When two or more 16th notes are joined together, a double beam is used, thus:

Relative Time Values

When Knighthood was in Flower

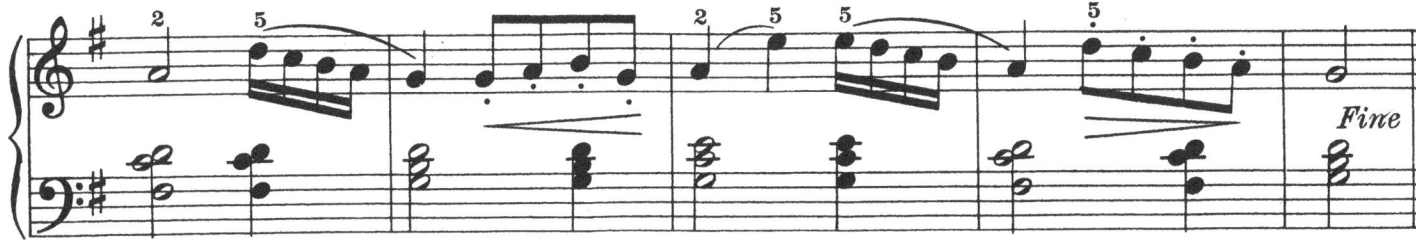

Syncopation

Westward Ho!

Leger Lines

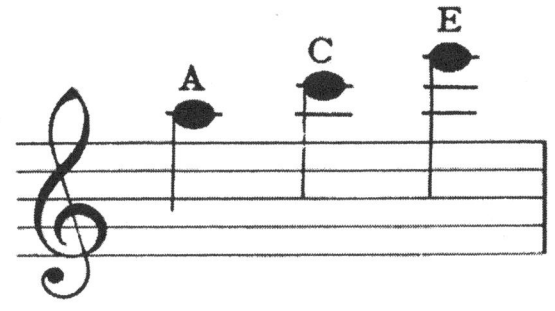
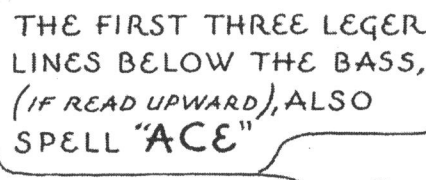
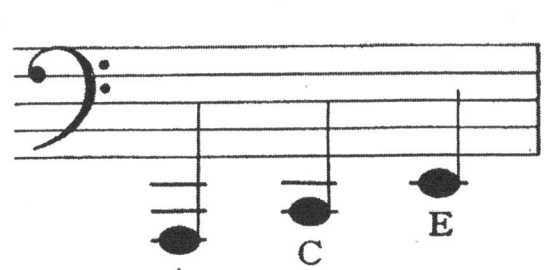
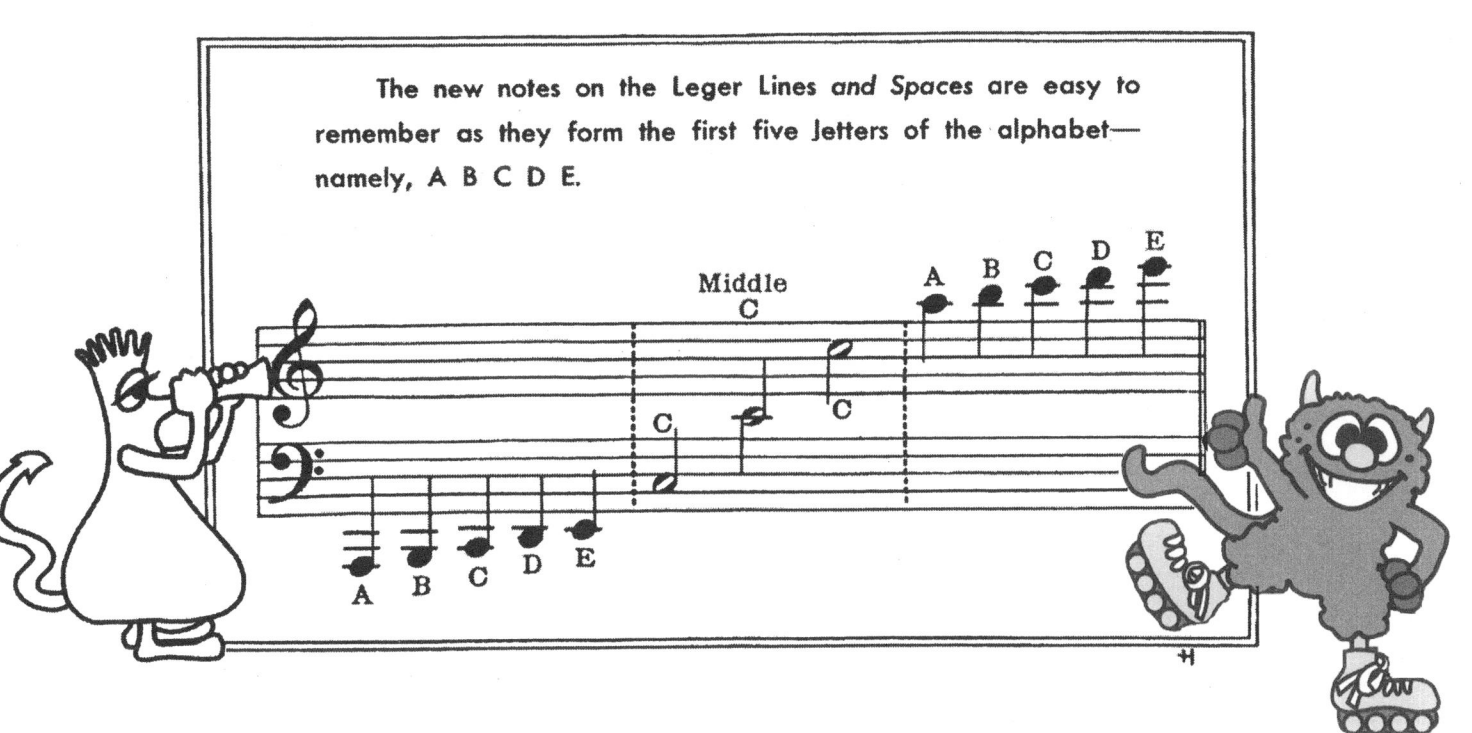

Leger Lines Below Bass Staff

By writing their letter names under certain bass notes, the following piece becomes much easier to read.

Dance of the Hobgoblins

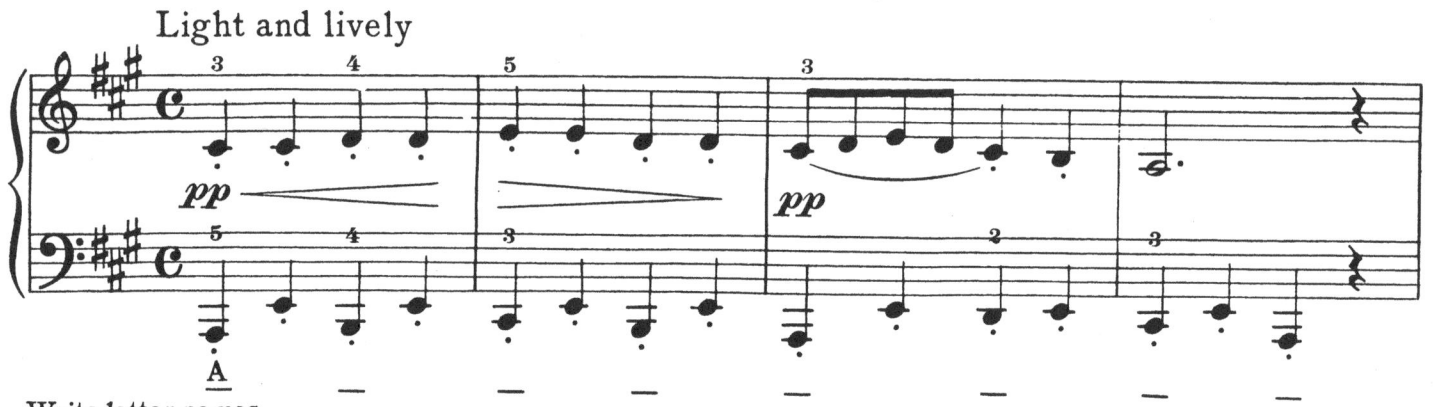

Write letter names where indicated.

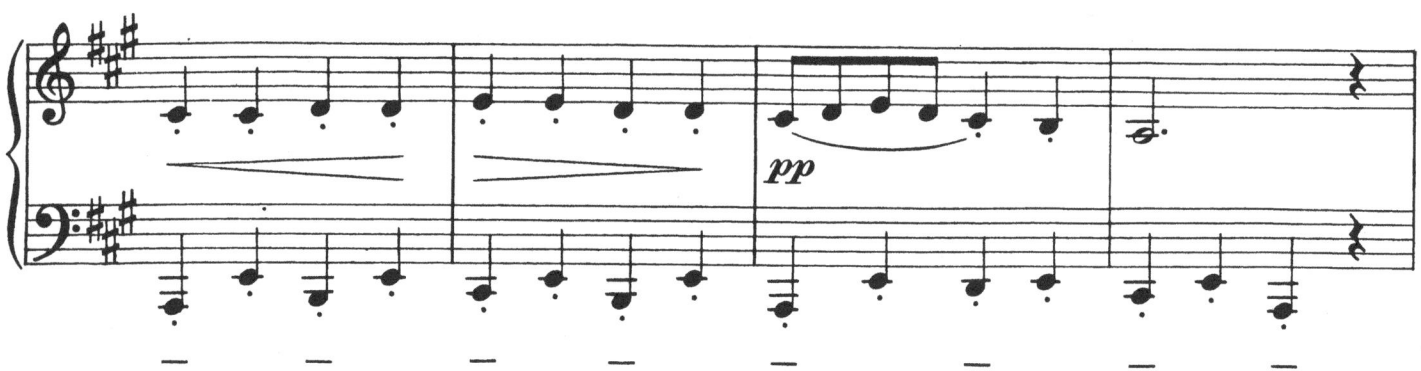

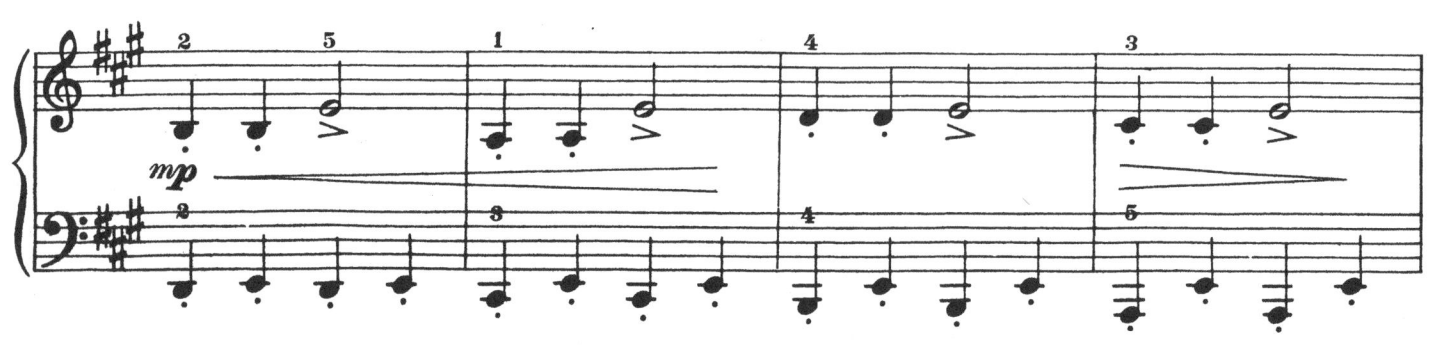

Grace Notes

There are several varieties of GRACE NOTES, but the one used most often looks like this. It has no set Time Value and should be "flipped" into the principal note (which follows) as quickly as possible.

The Campbells are Coming

Scotch Folk Tune

Staccato Playing

Mozart and his sister playing before Marie Theresa
From a painting by Borckmann

MOZART, one of the world's greatest musicians, began composing little pieces at the age of four. And when he was six he played in public concerts.

The example below, from the Opera, "The Magic Flute," affords fine study in staccato playing.

It is suggested that the right hand use wrist staccato for the single notes while the left hand plays the chords with forearm staccato.

from
"The Magic Flute"

W. A. Mozart
Adapted

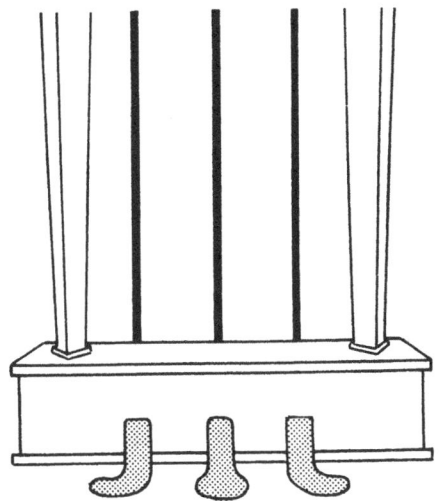

There are three pedals on the modern piano.

At present we shall use only the one on the right—the damper pedal.

It is sometimes (incorrectly!) called the *loud* pedal.

Actually it has nothing to do with the loudness of piano playing.

Its function is to sustain the tone by raising the dampers from the strings.

There are several markings in use to indicate the pedal.
In this book, this sign ⌊_____⌋ will be used.

The pedal is pressed down at the beginning and released immediately at the end of the sign.

Try it on the Pedal Study below and note how the bass tones continue to sing even though the left hand has passed over to play keys in the upper register.

Pedal Study

Broken Chords with Pedal

Over the Fence is Out!

The Pedal in Chord Playing

IN the following piece the CHORDS should sound as though they were played on a church organ. This means that each chord must be as sustained as possible, that is, one chord must be connected to the next by means of the PEDAL.

NOTE THE NEW PEDAL MARK!

This sign is used to show that the PEDAL is released and pressed down again *immediately* in order to preserve an unbroken legato, thus →

Sometimes you will see a pedal mark like this →

Or the word Ped. may be used like this →

Always remember that all three marks have the same **meaning**.

The Church Organ

Rapid Two-note Slurs

Be sure to apply the DROP-ROLL attack when playing the two-note slurs in this piece.

Since they are played rapidly, the UP stroke must be a very short one.

Just enough to release the last note of each slur and to drop in time on the next one.

Fun on the Beach

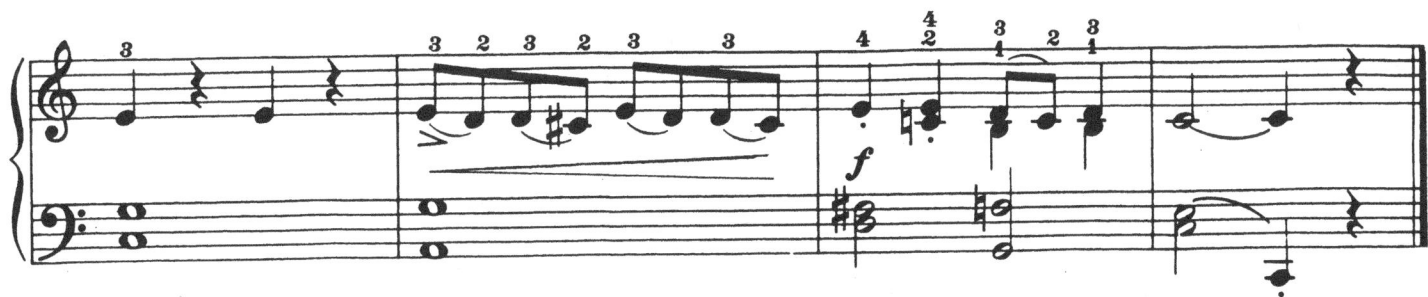

Johann Strauss, known as the "Waltz King," was born in Vienna in 1804.

He was a master of the Waltz form and wrote an astounding number of compositions, most of which are still popular.

from
The Emperor Waltz

Johann Strauss
Adapted

Through the Clouds

Moderato

Sixteenths in Four-Four

Etude

Moderato

Sixteenths in Two-Four

The Lonesome Stream

Moderato

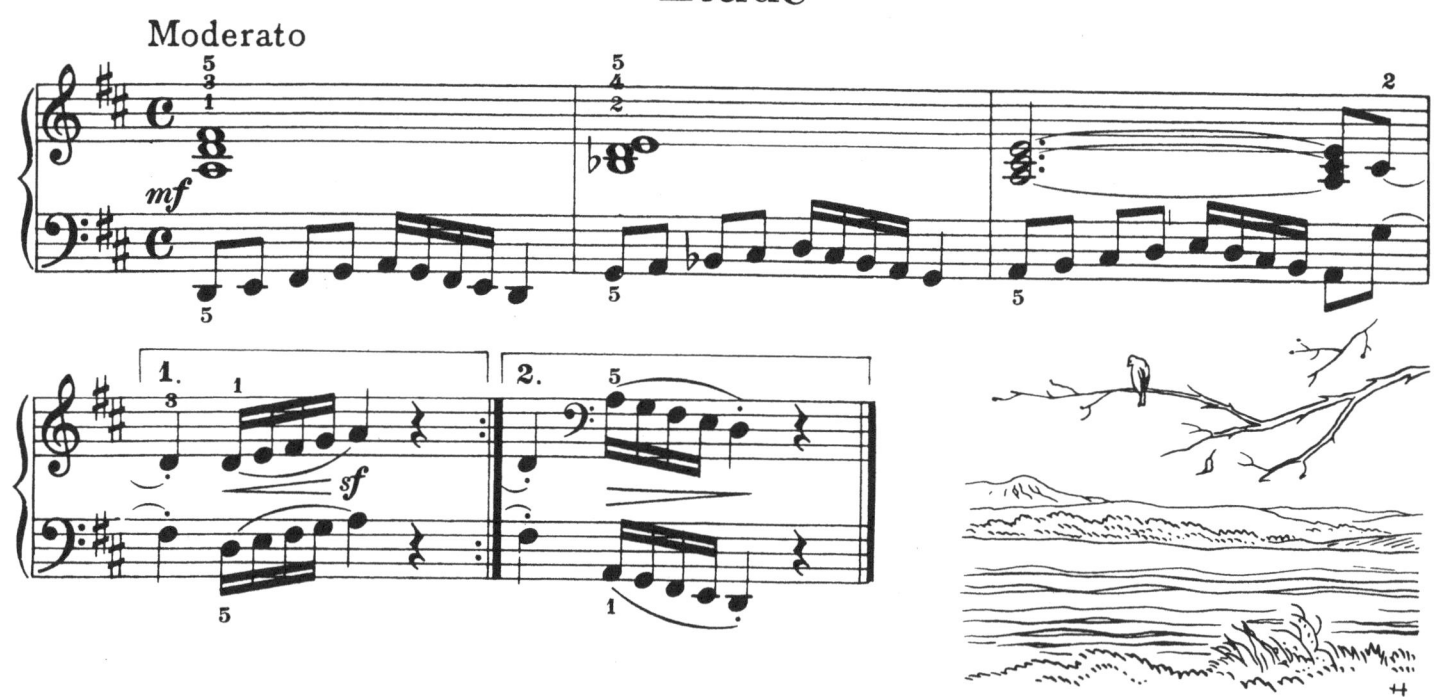

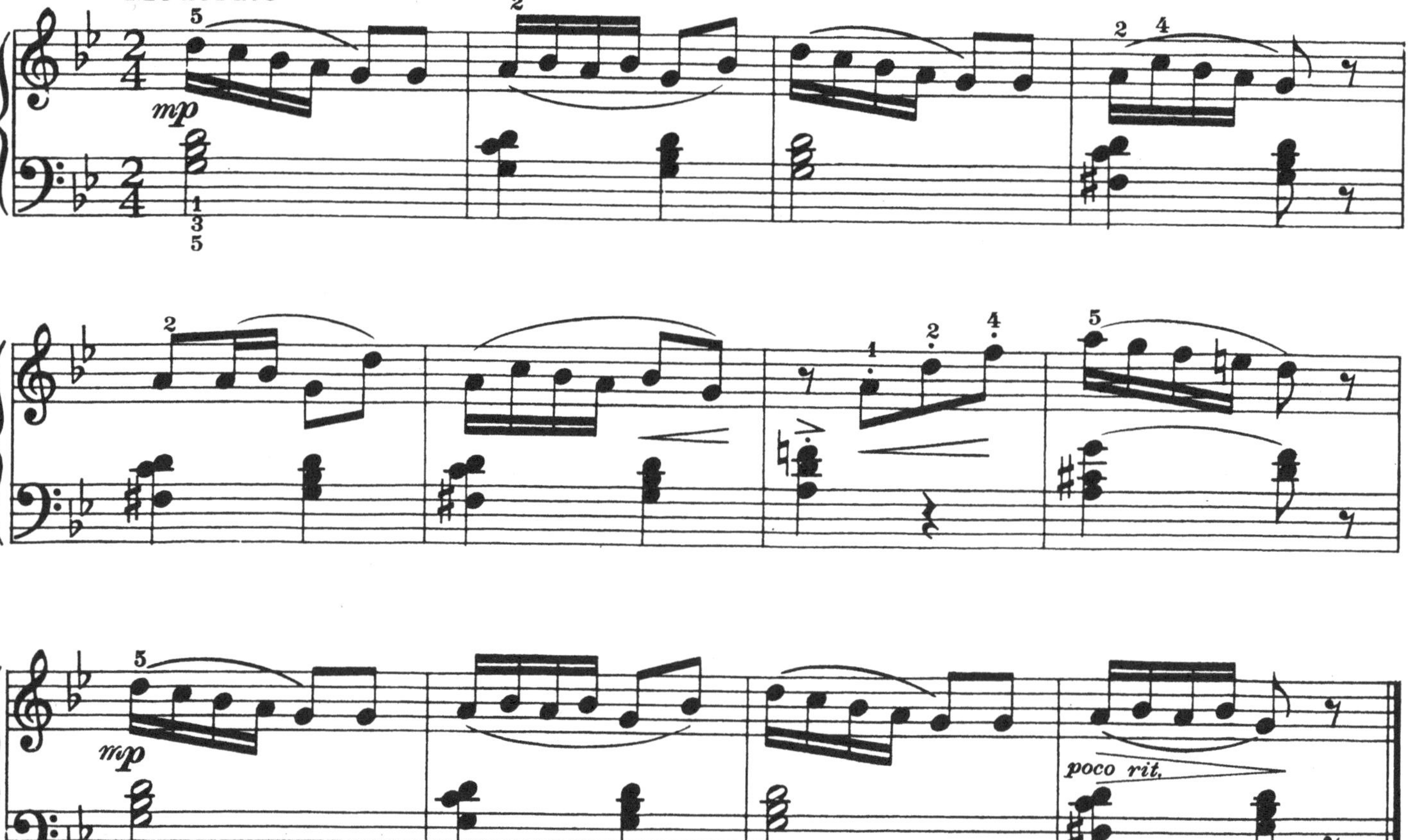

Sixteenths in Six-Eight

Etude

Moderato

Serenade

Allegretto

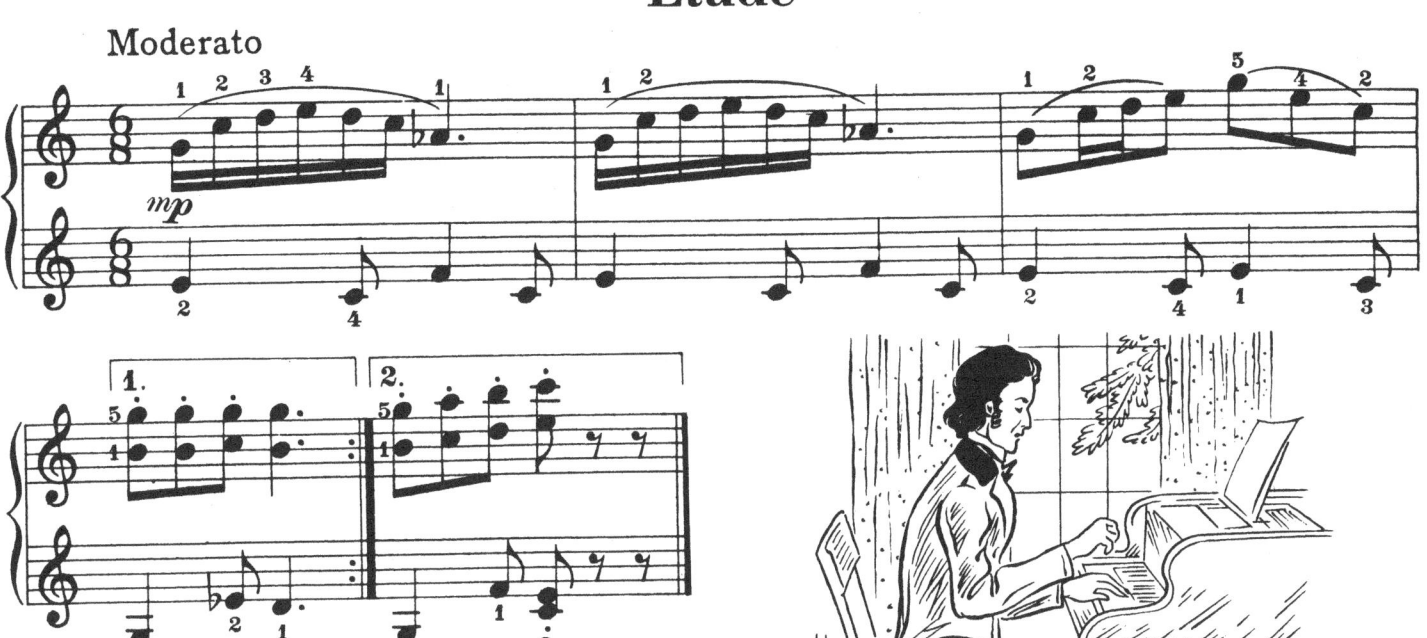

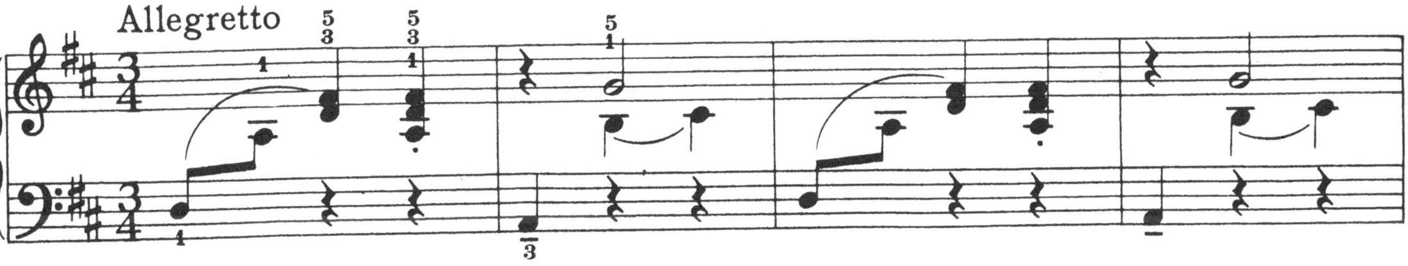

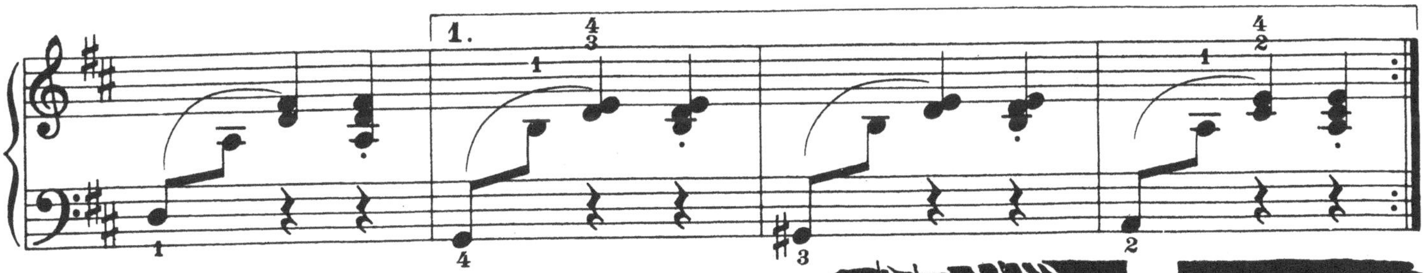

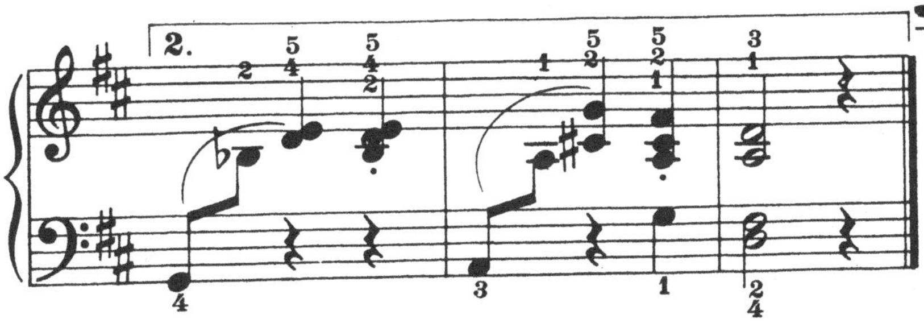

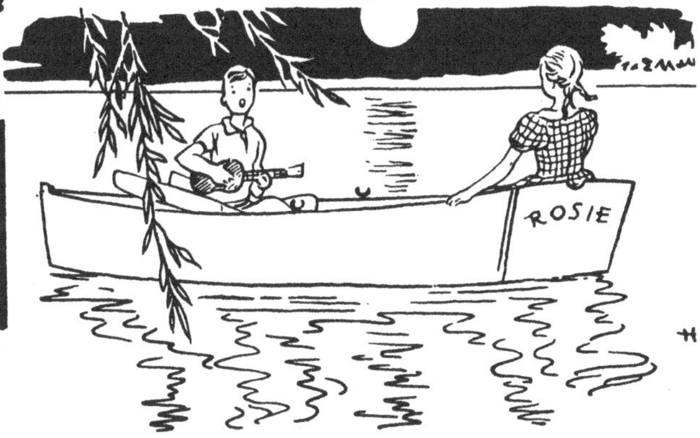

Broken Chords with Pedal

Old Faithful Geyser

The New Bike

Thumb Under and 2nd Finger Over

Hand in NORMAL five-finger position

Hand position with thumb UNDER the second finger

Before playing this piece, place your hand in position and practice the following exercise until the thumb can be passed under smoothly without turning the hand.

First each hand separately then together one octave apart.

Etude

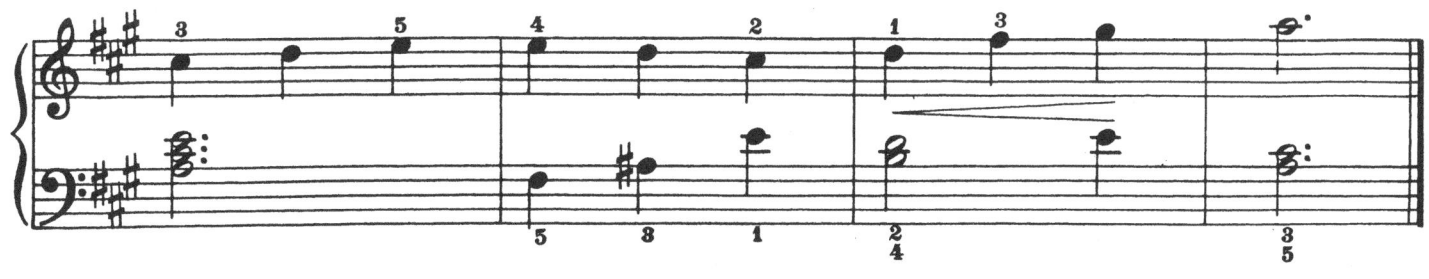

Whirling Propellers

Thumb under 3rd Finger

Passing the thumb under the 3rd finger requires a little more effort than in passing it under the 2nd.

It should be practiced over and over until the motion can be made smoothly *without turning the hand*.

Etude

3rd Finger over Thumb

Ballet Rehearsal

In the Days of Powdered Wigs
(Gavotte)

Legato and Staccato Contrast

The Tobacco Auctioneer

Allegro

Sold to A-mer-i-can!

Leger Lines
(Above Treble Staff)

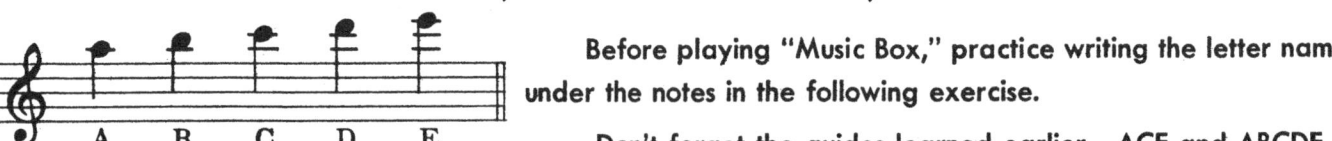

Before playing "Music Box," practice writing the letter names under the notes in the following exercise.

Don't forget the guides learned earlier—ACE and ABCDE.

Write the letter names

Music Box

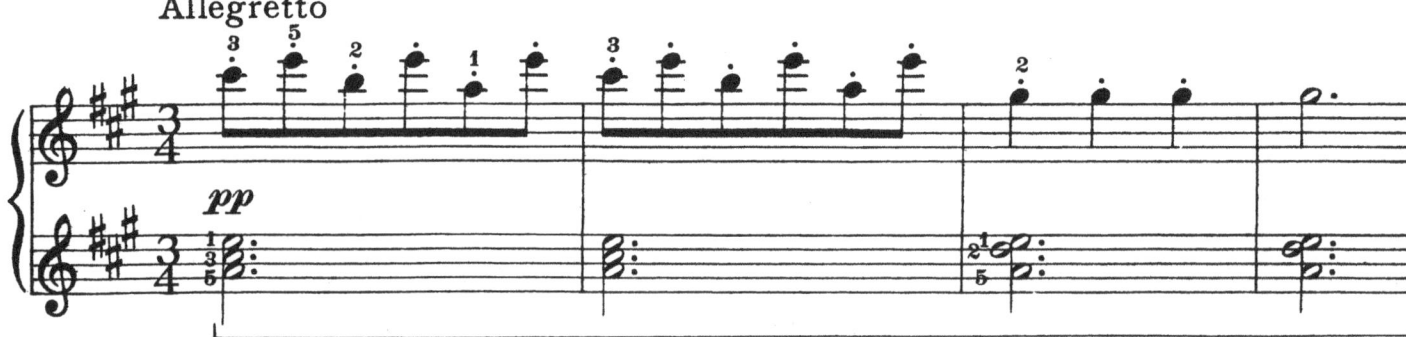

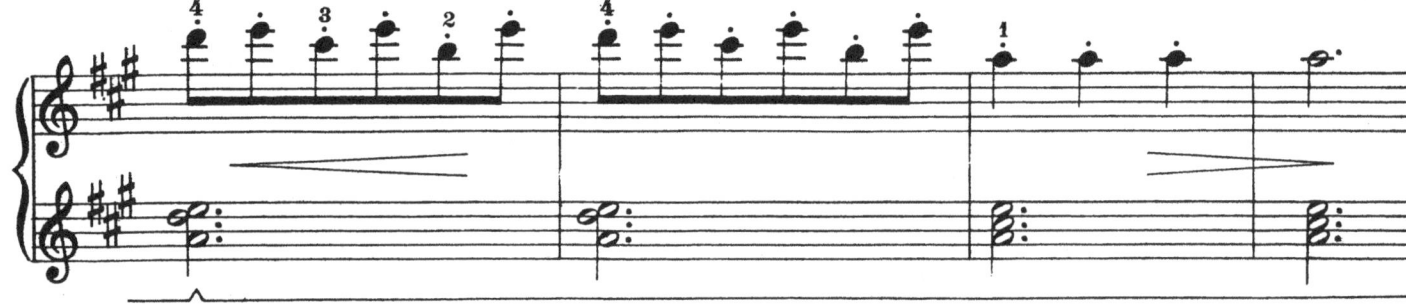

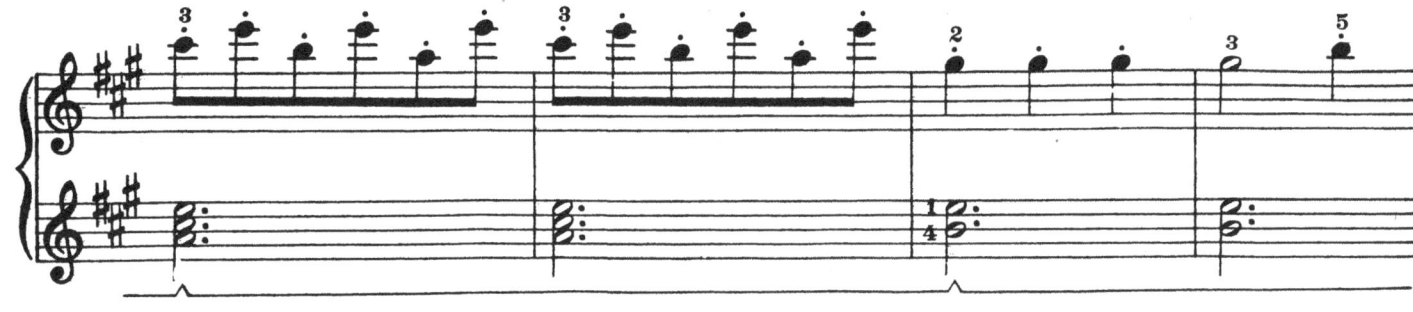

Transposition

A device often used in Popular Music is that of repeating a melody—moving up a half step at each repetition.

In the following example the melody first appears in the key of C Major.

It is then repeated in C# Major—half step higher.

It is again heard, this time in D Major—another half step higher.

The transposition will be easy if the same fingers are used in each key.

For exercise in transposition, you might try this with other tunes in the book.

Barn Dance

The Double Flat

The Double Flat sign (𝄫) is used to lower a note which is already flatted. In the following piece, because of the Key Signature, E is already flat. When it becomes necessary to lower this note, a double flat must be used. E double flat is, of course, the same key as D natural.

The use of double flats and double sharps has to do with correct musical spelling, something you will learn more about later.

This is an excellent piece upon which to practice transposition. Practice it therefore in G Major as well.

Use exactly the same fingers and remember that the *letter names* of the notes do not change. The only change necessary is that of Accidentals. To raise it a half step (G♭ to G), all Flats will become Naturals—all Naturals become Sharps—and the Double Flat becomes a single Flat.

Black Key Rag

The Caissons Go Rolling Along

General Edmund Gruber
(Adapted)

Allegro con brio

from
Danube Waves

J. Ivanovici
Adapted

41

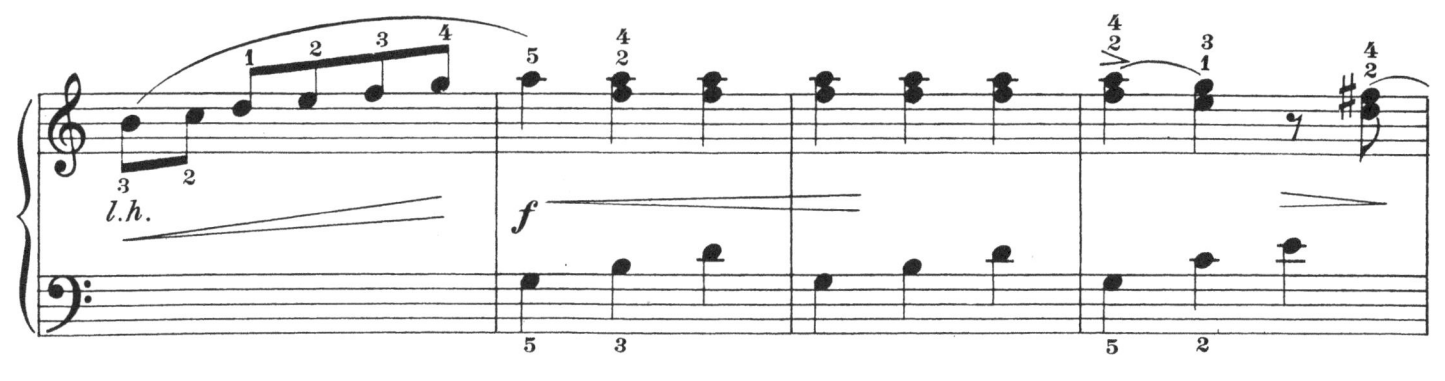

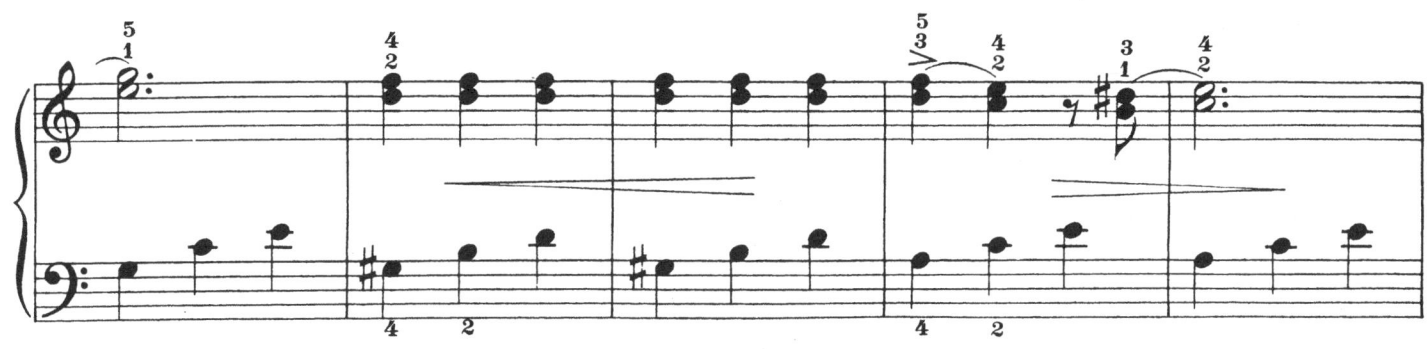

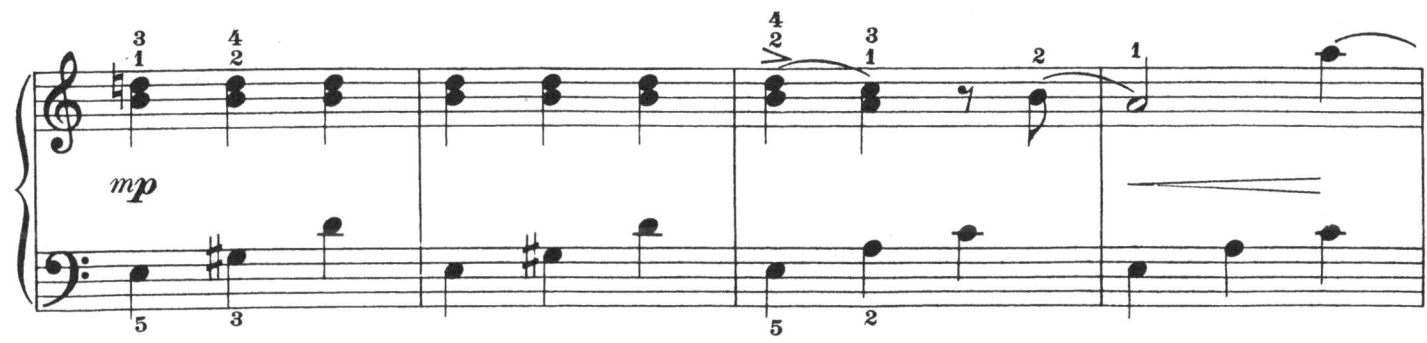

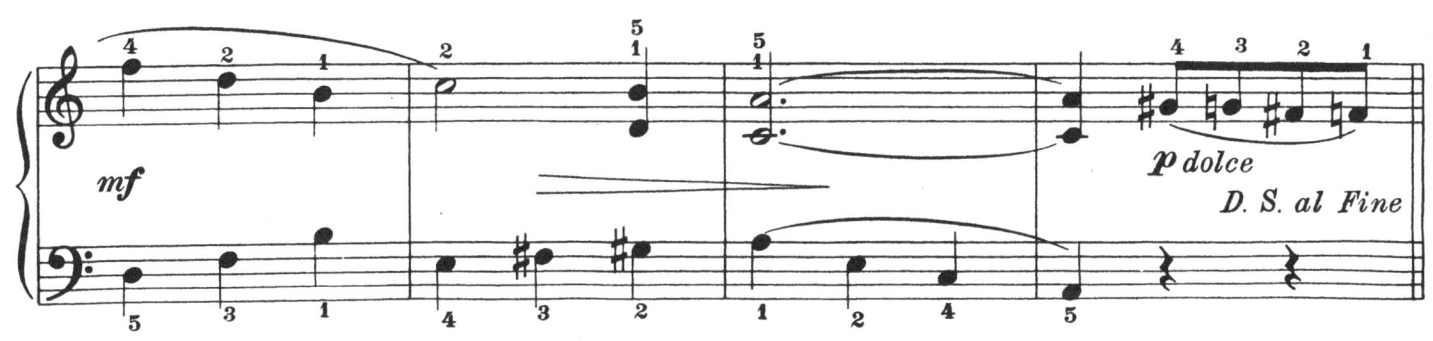

Study in Rhythm
Tango

Chord Playing
(Forearm Attack)

The School Song

FELIX MENDELSSOHN was one of the world's greatest composers. He wrote many compositions for piano, violin, voice and orchestra.

A great favorite among his smaller pieces was a set for piano which he called "Songs Without Words."

The following example, "Spring Song," is one of this set and has kept its popularity for many years.

from
Spring Song

Felix Mendelssohn

Certificate of Merit

This certifies that

....

has successfully completed

PART FIVE
OF
John Thompson's
EASIEST PIANO COURSE

and is eligible for promotion to

PART SIX

....
Teacher

Date..